**A Pillar Box Red Publication**

# we love you...

# N-DUBZ

## AN UNAUTHORISED 2012 ANNUAL

Written by: Sarah Delmege
Designed by: Nicky Regan

# CONTENTS

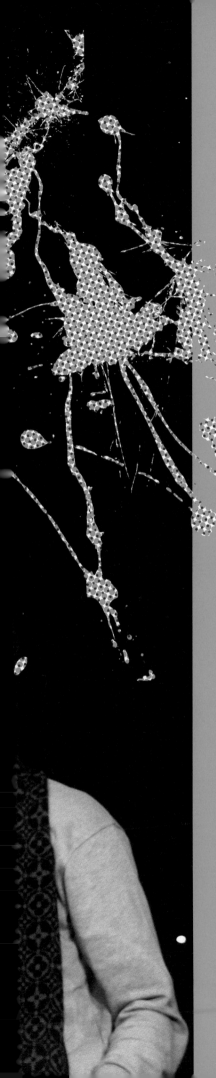

# we ♥ love you...
## N-DUBZ
### because...

...we could listen to your music all day and NEVER get bored...

...you are AMAZING live...

..you are a true family to each other...
... your trademark style! Na na niiiii!

...even though you are big-selling artists, you are still normal day-to-day people...

Dappy

*No doubt about it, N-Dubz are one of the UK's biggest bands. They are authentic, outspoken and raw. They were formed 11 years ago by Dappy's father, Byron Constavios.*

He recognized that the three school kids had raw talent and saw a way to keep them on the straight and narrow, away from the bad behaviour that surrounded them.

It took N-Dubz eight years to break through. Uncle B scraped together money with which to hire studio space and pay for three white-label albums. They wrote, they gigged and they recorded, developing their own original style, which was totally different from anything else already out there.

# HOW IT ALL BEGAN

*They're a hip-hop/R&B/multi-platform pop culture sensation. But how did the trio start?*

10

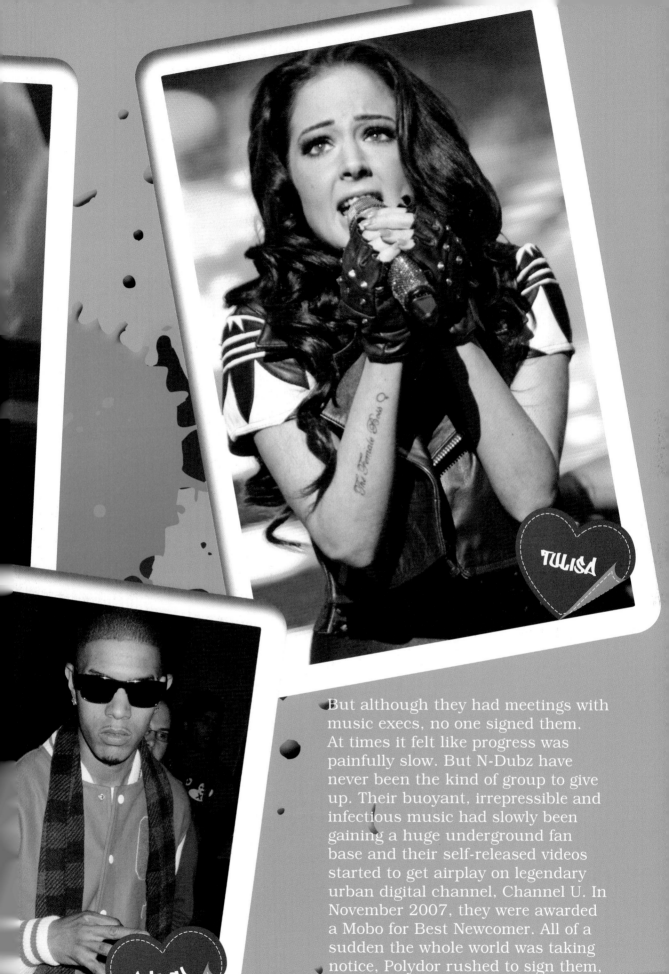

TULISA

FAZER

But although they had meetings with music execs, no one signed them. At times it felt like progress was painfully slow. But N-Dubz have never been the kind of group to give up. Their buoyant, irrepressible and infectious music had slowly been gaining a huge underground fan base and their self-released videos started to get airplay on legendary urban digital channel, Channel U. In November 2007, they were awarded a Mobo for Best Newcomer. All of a sudden the whole world was taking notice, Polydor rushed to sign them, and their single, *'You Better Not Waste My Time,'* was released.

N-Dubz were on their way.     *cont...*

They were soon re-signed to All Around The World – a subsidiary of the same parent company, Universal. As Tulisa says, *"You can't wait for things to happen, you have to make them happen."*

Just a few years after the debut album that marked them out as one of the world's premiere hip-hop groups, they've broken new ground, staging the first ever arena tour by a British urban band.

FANZ

They've got a devoted fan base, triple-platinum albums, sell-out tours, a best-selling book and *Being N-Dubz*, a massively successful documentary series under their belt.

As artists, they know they have to keep evolving and doing new things to keep themselves and their fans happy. They're always looking for the next step, they know they've got to keep pushing themselves forward, but they'll always be N-Dubz, no matter what happens, with that distinctive N-Dubz sound.

N-DUBZ

FANZ

**Name:** Tula 'Tulisa' Contostavlos

**DOB:** 13 July 1988

**Hometown:** Camden

**Early Days:** An only child, Tulisa became a carer for her mother from an early age. Having survived the toughest of childhoods, Tulisa found escape first as a solo artist, then alongside Dappy and Fazer in what was then called the Lickle Rinsers Crew, later to become N-Dubz. Together, they would travel the the road to superstardom from Camden Town by way of America and beyond...

Tulisa, with her unique voice, has frequently been heard in the role of radio broadcaster, and she has also carved out a successful career as an actress with roles in Channel 4's Dubplate Drama and in movies such as Bulla. And let's not forget being a judge on *The X Factor*!

**Did you know?** *She loves pizza!*

ALL ABOUT TULISA

**Name:** Richard Rawson AKA Fazer

**DOB:** 5 February 1987

**Hometown:** Camden

**Early Days:** After an early meeting with Dappy, they soon became schoolmates, and were later joined by a young Tulisa. Fazer's talents as a record producer emerged at a young age on tracks such as *Everyday of My Life* and *Life is Getting Sicker by the Day*, and would provide him with his key role in the N-Dubz line-up.

Fazer has collaborated with leading UK artists including Ransome, Paper Pablo, Bashy, Ice Kid, Giggs, Chipmunk and Griminal. He also had a brief flirtation with acting, alongside his N-Dubz bandmates in Channel 4's Dubplate Drama.

**Did you know:** Fazer appeared as a dancer in a video for a K.I.G. song, *Head, Shoulders, Kneez and Toez*.

FA Take It Easy!

ALL ABOUT FAZER

18

**Name:** Costadinos 'Dino' Contostavlos

**DOB:** 11 June 1987

**Hometown:** Camden

**Early Days:** Performing gigs around Camden from the young age of 12 under the group name Lickle Rinsers Crew, the band soon built a reputation and a following and their path to stardom began.

He's collaborated with Chipmunk, Fearless, Gracious K, Skepta, Tinchy Stryder and many other groundbreaking artists on the vibrant UK hip-hop, grime & R&B scene.

A deadly lyricist with razor sharp delivery and flow, he's also an accomplished singer/song-writer and producer, and has a unique style that has become a trademark.

He is famous for his taste in headwear; especially his trademark knitted Peruvian hats.

**Did you know:** Dappy supports Arsenal

D-A-P-'s to the Y!

ALL ABOUT DAPPY

we ♥love♥ you...

LIVE ON STAGE

WHICH BIT OF N-DUBZ CREW ARE YOU?

*Were you born to be an A-lister like Dappy, Fazer and Tulisa or are you happier behind the scenes?*

**1. Whenever you get your photo taken, you always...**

a. Drag a friend into the shot with you for moral support.

b. Pull a comedy face.

c. Turn your face away or hide behind someone else.

**2. During a lesson, you're asked to read your homework out loud. Do you...**

a. Jump up and give it all you've got.

b. Panic and pretend you've suddenly lost your voice to get out of it.

c. Just act as if you're talking to a friend and calmly get on with it.

**3. When you're not at school, you love to...**

a. Listen to music in your room and chat to your friends.

b. Practice singing or rehearse your lines for drama club.

c. Get together with friends and get all the latest gossip.

**4. The celebrity lady you most admire is...**

a. Kirsten Stewart. She just wears whatever she's comfy in.

b. Pixie Lott. She's always fashionable but not too flashy.

c. Lady Gaga. She always stands out from the crowd.

**5. If you had to ask your crush out, you'd prefer to do it...**

a. Over the phone.

b. In person and in private.

c. In class. You're at your best when you've got an audience.

**6. The school paper wants to do a feature on you. Do you...**

a. Tell them everything they want to know.

b. Offer to get them an interview with the class hottie instead.

c. Tell them your best friend is much more up for this kind of thing.

*Add up your scores:*

a) 2 b) 3 c) 1
a) 3 b) 1 c) 2
a) 1 b) 3 c) 2
a) 1 b) 2 c) 3
a) 1 b) 2 c) 3
a) 3 b) 2 c) 1

*For answers see page 61.*

*Tulisa has shone as a judge on the X Factor – wowing the audience, contestants and fellow judges. She was understandably a little shaky about joining the X Factor, but her N-Dubz experience definitely qualified her to do a good job.*

Not only is she drop dead gorgeous, she's been through all kinds of struggles to get to the top.

In many ways she's very similar to her predecessor, Cheryl Cole.

They're both smart and sassy and certainly both have the same wow factor. And Cheryl herself was fully behind Tulisa's new job, sending her a huge bunch of flowers to wish her good luck and even inviting Tulisa to her birthday party, where the two danced the night away.

And contrary to reports, the N-Dubz boys are really proud of their bandmate, and reckon her new job shows just how far the band have come.

# TULISAS'S GOT THE X-FACTOR

we love you...
N-DUBZ

DRAKE

NAS

TUPAC

STING

PHIL

DAPPY AND FAZER'S
INSPIRATIONS

# 9 THINGS YOU DIDN'T KNOW

* Tulisa's favourite thing is smelling a kitchen full of food.

* Dappy once played noughts and crosses on Fazer's face while he was sleeping!

* Tulisa is the mother hen of the group and regularly bosses the boys around!

* Fazer once had to be escorted out of the Westfield Shopping Centre because his fans went crazy.

* Tulisa played Tallulah in her school production of Bugsy Malone.

* *Ouch* got nine million hits on YouTube in one month!

* Tulisa hates spending over £50 on clothes.

* Dappy reckons the best place to take a girl on a date is McDonalds.

* Seari 4 realli!

*"Always follow your own path."*

**FAZER**

*"We are a true family."*

**FAZER**

*"I just wanna climb into the crowd and give them all a group hug."*

**FAZER**

*"We Love our little N-Dublets."*

**TULISA**

*"It's mad to think some people see me as a heart-throb. It's just me innit."*

**DAPPY**

*"Learning gives you options and options are always good!"*

**DAPPY**

# SAY WHAT?

# N-DUBZ STYLE

## Fazer Stylin'

Fazer has developed his own sense of style, and has been seen rocking everything from Adidas Originals to Two Angle on a regular basis.

His hip hop style is instantly recognizable. Fazer recently went on a London shopping trip and popped on his trademark baseball cap. "All of a sudden people all over the shopping centre were looking at me. The whole store entrance was backed up with people," he laughs.

Unlike most other celebs, N-Dubz won't hear of shops being kept open especially for them so they can browse in private. They're still from North London and wouldn't dream of inconveniencing anybody or acting like super stars.

*Duku Fazer!*

## Dappy Stylin'

Dappy has a huge love for what he describes as 'eye-catching headwear'. He's never seen without one of his vast selection of woolly chullos, turning up the right or left earflap of the hat.

Dappy definitely has a refreshing and unique take on streetfashion and always stands out from the crowd, looking effortlessly cool.

Recently he's been inspired to wear more tailored suits and smart jackets, although he still wouldn't be without his beloved Adidas. "You have to evolve," says the star.

*Nice hats / whatever!*

*She's the North London estate girl who never forgets her tough roots. She's certainly not a slave to designer clothes, wowing in the fashion stakes with her high street style.*

Whether in a loosely fitting jumpsuit or a bodycon dress, she can wear old skool or contemporary cool and always looks like a million dollars. She's often seen wearing the likes of Matalan, River Island and Topshop. She wears exactly what she wants and always stands out from the crowd.

One thing's for sure: Tulisa really does know how to take celebrity fashion to a new level.

# TULISA'S STYLE

we ♥ love you...
N-DUBZ

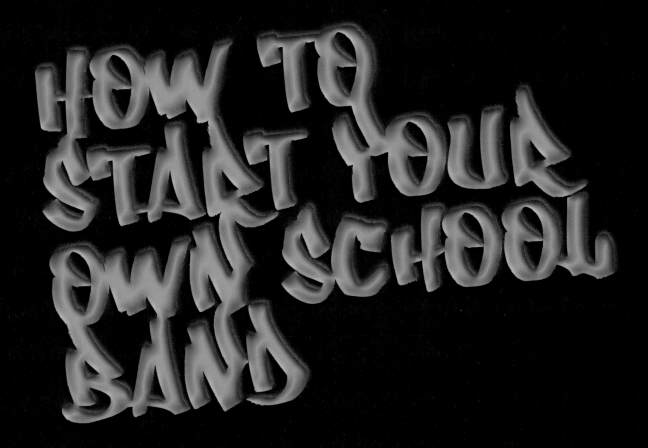

# HOW TO START YOUR OWN SCHOOL BAND

***Follow these easy steps and you could be the next N-Dubz!***

Find the rest of the band. Think about whether anyone will be playing instruments and work out who'll play what. (Oh and make sure they can actually play the instruments too!) Take some time to work out what kind of music you'll play. If you're into all types of music, like N-Dubz, a mish-mash of styles could totally work!

Choose a cool name for the band. A lot of bands go through several different names before sticking to one. N-Dubz were called The Lickle Rinsers Crew and NW1 before hitting on N-Dubz.

Practice, practice, practice. A lot. Have at least one practice session a week.

Make sure you have a space or place to practice in.

Create a band page on Myspace or Facebook as a way of promoting your music and getting more fans.

Once you've got some good songs and are feeling confident performing together, try and get a gig lined up. Could you play at your school? Zoop. Zoop.

Don't give up! And make sure you still do your homework – Tulisa, Dappy and Fazer are all about getting homework done.

Na Na Niiii!

# A–Z of N-DUBZ

**A *is for*** Are you suuuuuuuuuick!

**B *is for*** Best UK Act and Best Album.

**C *is for*** Camden, the N-Dubz 'hood.

**D *is for*** Dappy.

**E *is for*** Every Day of My Life.

**F *is for*** Fazer.

**G *is for*** Gary Barlow, friend and muse.

**H *is for*** Hats.

**I *is for*** I Swear.

**J *is for*** Jez Welahm the first DJ to back N-Dubz on radio.

**K *is for*** Karate – how Dappy and Fazer first met.

L *is for* Lickle Rinsers Crew.

M *is for* MC.

N *is for* NaNaNiiiii!

O *is for* Ouch!

P *is for* Polydor.

Q *is for* Queen. Fazer loves them.

R *is for* ROAR Global.

S *is for* Studio.

T *is for* Tulisa.

U *is for* Uncle B.

V *is for* Vocalist.

W *is for* What is the World Coming To, N-Dubz's first ever song.

X *is for* X Factor.

Y *is for* YouTube.

Z *is for* Zoop Zoop!

Papa / Changed / Na / Thought

If / Story / Ever / Get / You / Not

The / You / Ever / That / Better

Better / Can / My / Na / Breaking / Ever

Hear / Heart / Na / Never / It / My

Time / Me / Is / Niiiii / I / Would / Waste

*Answers on Page 61.*

Can you work out the
5 N-Dubz lyrics that
these words make up?
It's Maddas 4 rallies!

SCRAMBLED
LYRICS

**Mr Hudson**

Tulisa: *"Mr Hudson is hilarious. He's such a strange and intriguing character, unlike anyone else I have ever met."*

Fazer: *"He's just too talented. I respect him in a big way."*

**Gary Barlow**

Dappy: *"He approached us because he liked what we were doing. We respect him for taking time out of his heavy schedule to come and write with underdogs like us."*

Tulisa: *"He's got this laid-back kind of vibe, and he's so talented."*

# COLLABORATIONS

**Chipmunk**

Fazer: *"As a young lyricist Chipmunk is still developing but his ability is already phenomenal."*

Dappy: *"He's a huge star."*

Tulisa: *"He's got a light in him that shows he's one of those people who's good inside."*

**Dream Collaboration**

Fazer: *"There's one big dream collaboration that I want to put in place. I don't even care if I'm on the record. I'll just make the music. I wanna see Dappy, Akon, R Kelly and Eminem all with their unique voices on a record. That would be sick."*

Dappy: *"Akon and Drake are two artists who immediately spring to mind."*

EMINEM

GARY B

R KELLY

AKON

**1. What is Dappy's real name?**

a. Dino Contostavlos

b. Richard Contostavlos

c. Gino Rawson

**2. What is N-Dubz's home-town?**

a. Chelmsford

b. Harlow

c. Camden

**3. Which N-Dubz song did Wiley feature in?**

a. Playing With Fire

b. Number One

c. Na Na

**4. What type of clothing is Dappy most famous for?**

a. His colourful sunglasses

b. His knitted hats

c. His designer t-shirts

**5. Which single was nominated for a Brit Award in 2010?**

a. Ouch

b. You better not waste my time

c. Number 1

**6. Which series did all three of the N-Dubz crew star in, but not as themselves?**

a. Skins

b. Dubplate Drama

c. Misfits

**7. Which country are Dappy and Tulisa's family originally from?**

a. Italy

b. Albania

c. Greece

**8. Which N-Dubz track was dedicated to Dappy's late father, Byron?**

a. Papa can you hear me?

b. Wouldn't you?

c. Strong again

**9. Which country do N-Dubz head to in series 2 of their reality show, Being N-Dubz?**

a. America

b. Russia

c. China

**Answers on page 61.**

# N-DUBZ
## TRIVIA QUIZ.

Think you know
N-Dubz inside out?
Take our tricky quiz
to find out.

# HOMETOWN FACTS

* Camden Town is an inner-city district in the London Borough of Camden.

* It's the rock 'n' roll heart of London and thousands of tourists flock there every year.

* The area is a hub of all things alternative such as goth, punk and emo.

* The Camden market is world famous and one of the biggest in Europe.

* Camden has some of the wealthiest neighbourhoods in London and some of the most deprived.

* Other famous people from Camden include Loose Women presenter Carol McGiffen, poet Dylan Thomas and Orlando Bloom.

**Are u suuuuuuuuuuuuuuick:** *That's amazing.*

**Duku Yourself:** *Big up yourself.*

**D-A-P-'s to the Y:** *Dappy.*

**Seari 4 realli:** *Are you being serious?*

**Bang bang shoes/whatever:** *Nice shoes/whatever.*

**FA Take it Easy:** *Fazer.*

**Maddas 4 rallies:** *That's proper mad.*

**Na Na:** *Both hi and goodbye.*

**Zoop zoop:** *An expression of excitement about anything.*

**Shabarky:** *Someone's eyeing you up.*

**A pinky:** *A £50 note.*

**N-Dublets:** *N-Dubz fans.*

**Weeeeeeeeeeeeee!:** *Use it to embarrass someone if you catch them out.*

**Say something:** *What you gonna do about it? A way to end a conversation.*

**Ha ha:** *Official N-Dubz trademark.*

**NaNaNiiiiii:** *Official N-Dubz trademark.*

N-DUBZ LANGUAGE

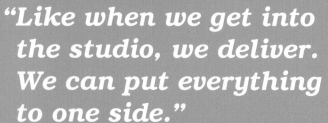

*"Like when we get into the studio, we deliver. We can put everything to one side."*

### Always be kind

*Tulisa:* "As well as trust, making an effort is the most important thing in a friendship – caring for someone and being there when necessary. If one of my friends was ill and by herself I would go round and cook her a meal or whatever. It's the little things that mean the most."

### Keep some stuff private

*Dappy:* "I'd tell Fazer anything, but everyone doesn't have to know all of your business. You don't want to put all your business up on Facebook or whatever."

### Don't lie

*Fazer:* "People who lie are out of order. I have no time for liars or anyone with a hidden agenda."

*Tulisa:* "Most of the time you don't need to lie. If you're worried you might hurt anyone's feelings then don't say anything. I don't like to talk too much about people. If I don't necessarily like someone, I'd rather not talk about them at all."

### Forgive and make up

*Dappy:* "Like when we get into the studio, we deliver. We can put everything to one side."

**"If one of my friends was ill and by herself I would go round and cook her a meal or whatever."**

Right now, the future's so bright, Tulisa, Dappy and Fazer must be pinching themselves on a regular basis to make sure they're not dreaming.

The band members are concentrating on their individual endeavours. Dappy's working on his solo projects. Fazer plans to sign new artists and develop talent. Tulisa is busy in the studios in between her X Factor gig and releasing her fragrances.

Every day is part of a new journey for Tulisa, Dappy and Fazer – they are still developing. The road ahead of them seems endless and there's no area in which they can't make their mark and influencing a whole new generation along the way.

# RIGHT HERE, RIGHT NOW

**The world won't have to wait long for the return of N-Dubz.**

They're in no doubt that a lot of hard work lies ahead. It may be hard to reach the top but things don't get any easier once you're there. Having succeeded, the pressure is on to keep succeeding. But N-Dubz wouldn't change a single thing.

The drive for the band comes from always remembering where they come from. They don't take anything for granted and they know they have to work every single day to deserve it. They still have a lot to give their N-Dublets and we can't wait to hear it.

Na Na!

P48
# TRIVIA QUIZ

1.  a
2.  c
3.  c
4.  b
5.  c
6.  b
7.  c
8.  a
9.  a

P44-45
# SCRAMBLED LYRICS

1. Papa if you can hear me
   (PAPA, CAN YOU HEAR ME)

2. The story changed my heart is breaking
   (OUCH)

3. Na na na na niiiii!
   (AGAINST ALL ODDS)

4. I never ever ever ever thought that it would ever get better
   (STRONG AGAIN)

5. You better not waste my time
   (YOU BETTER NOT WASTE MY TIME)

# QUIZ ANSWERS

## WHICH BIT OF N-DUBZ CREW ARE YOU?

### 13 and over: Future Superstar

Move over N-Dubz, there's a new diva in town. You love entertaining people and being centre stage – which is exactly where you want to be. You're never shy and you always take every opportunity to get yourself in the limelight. Stardom beckons.

### 7-12: Future Sound Mixer

You're more comfortable being yourself than putting on an act to entertain people. Although you'll find a little bit of fame fun, you'd prefer to produce music for superstars rather than be one yourself.

### 11 and under: Future Roadie

The idea of everyone gossiping about you fills you with dread. Your shyness may stop you aiming for superstardom, and you'd be happiest behind the scenes helping the band set up for gigs.